Contents

Meet Our Writer

Anne E. Wimberly
Dr. Anne Wimberly is an associate professor of Christian educa-
tion and church music at The Interdenominational Theological
Center in Atlanta, GA. She has a Master of Theological Studies
degree from Garrett Evangelical Theological Seminary and a
Ph.D. in Educational Leadership from Georgia State University.

Introduction

T his study book is a part of a series called The Bible People. This book is among the first four books we are producing at this time. They are: Bible Disciples, Bible Prophets, Bible Women, and Bible Missionaries. Hopefully, other titles will follow under other groupings.

We are aware of the cases where one person can fit in more than one grouping. A person can be a disciple as well as a missionary. A person who is a woman can also be in the grouping of prophets. Nevertheless, we are highlighting one aspect of that person's ministry in this series. It may be surprising to some readers to find out that a particular person is put in a grouping they never thought he or she belonged to. Our attempt here is to see that person from a different angle and perspective than we have generally seen in the past. But then, some persons will be in their unique ministry.

Each book at present has seven sessions on seven (or more) persons. Obviously, this is not an exhaustive list but rather a selective list of Bible people in a given category. Some of them have a large body of information and the others have very little, but we will still be able to learn valuable traits of their ministry and the impact they had in their own time and world.

In a few cases, two persons are studied in the same session because they belonged together as husband and wife (Priscilla and Aquila) or mother-in-law and daughter-in-law (Naomi and Ruth) or sisters (Mary and Martha). They jointly witnessed or created situations that impacted the history of the community in which they lived. That history has become the history of our faith and their impact has affected us as followers of the Way which God has shown us in and through Jesus Christ, who is our Savior and Lord.

We believe that these studies of the Bible People will renew our faith, strengthen our resolve to become worthy sons and daughters of God, and transform us into lighthouses and torches to give hope to the lost, and light to those in darkness.

Statement of Purpose: The purpose of these studies is to help us learn from the lives and ministries of some of the people in the Bible who have made a significant impact on the community of their time and who have contributed toward God's design for a God-centered life for all people, including us.

QuickLead®

This QUICK information will help you effectively LEAD a session of *Bible People*, either in a class setting or for your personal study. On *Bible People* pages look for the following:

ICONS

Six icons show you at a glance what kind of activity you are asked to do, such as reflection, group discussion, or interaction. See page 4 for more specific information about the icons.

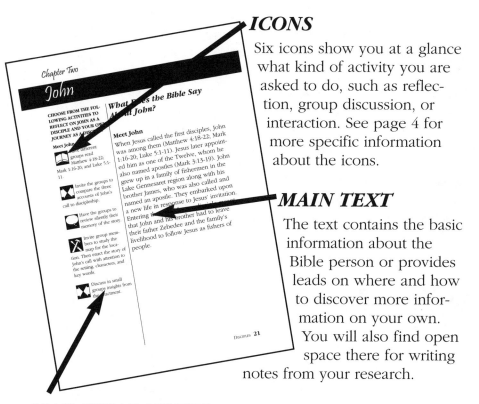

MAIN TEXT

The text contains the basic information about the Bible person or provides leads on where and how to discover more information on your own. You will also find open space there for writing notes from your research.

MARGINAL NOTES

Instructions for leading the session or for your own personal study are found in the margins. Questions for reflection or discussion are here too.

For more information, read the *series introductions* and the other articles in this issue of *Bible People*.

Icons

Icons are picture/symbols that show you at a glance what you should do with different parts of the main text or learning options during a reflection or study session in the *Bible People* series. The six kinds of icons are

Discussion—Either the main text or a marginal note will suggest discussion questions or discussion starters.

Group Interaction—Either the main text or a marginal note will provide instructions for how to do a group activity that requires more interplay among group members than a discussion.

Bible Study—Individuals studying *Bible People* are encouraged to dig into the Bible and mine the Scriptures to learn more about the Bible person and his or her contribution to the faith. Bible study may be done in a group or on your own.

Bible Tools—*Bible People* uses the "discovery" method of teaching, using various Bible reference tools, such as dictionaries, commentaries, atlases, and concordances. Activities that require more than the Bible will be identified with this icon. (See pages 5-7 on "The Discovery Method" and the inside back cover for "Bible Reference Tools")

Reflection—Group or individual *Bible People* students will have opportunities to think over questions, information, new insights, assumptions, and learnings. On occasion, the text will provide open space for written reflections.

Worship—Sessions may begin or end with time for corporate or private devotions.

The Bible Discovery Method™ of Study

We are made in the image of God, and we yearn for God. Sometimes that is where our similarities end! As unique individuals in search of a relationship with the divine, we come to the task in ways as diverse as humankind. Each of us has a particular and personal perspective on the Scriptures because of our individual experiences. Our acquaintance with the Bible is influenced by our general attitude about what the Bible is and how it is to be used, as well as by a host of other factors. Each of us learns in our own way; some by doing, others by listening, others by watching, yet others by figuring out for themselves.

Discovering the Bible

There is no single "right" way to learn, although much published curricula and many Bible study teachers depend on a few tried methods, particularly lecture, reading from study books, and group discussion. While there is certainly value in these educational practices, a more interactive or personally invested approach often helps a lesson "stick" better. Persons remember best what they experience the most intimately.

The *Bible People* series study depends on what we are calling the "discovery" method. Rather than providing all the background information about a Bible person, we are inviting you as learners to do some of your own digging, through

- the Scriptures
- Bible commentaries
- Bible dictionaries
- Key word or topical concordances
- and other Bible reference materials.

The items selected for further study can be found in most basic Bible resources. You do not need to have a specific dictionary or commentary. Most of these reference materials may be available in your church library.

Three Main Questions

The sessions are organized around three main questions:
- What does the Bible say about the person?
- What else would we like to know about the Bible person?
- How does what I know about the Bible person affect my life and faith?

Throughout the session you will discover what some or all of the references to each Bible person say and mean. Some information will be provided directly. Other information will come to you through your own discovery, perhaps by
- looking at maps;
- looking up key words in a concordance and then finding the appropriate passages;
- researching a specific Bible reference in a commentary;
- reading entries about key words, concepts, or persons in a Bible dictionary.

All of these activities can be done in a personal, self-study setting; most will also lend themselves to group work and discussion. The length of your study session can be adapted to the time you wish to spend in exploration.

Answering the Questions

In some cases, the biblical information is abundant. In others, the Scriptures may mention only a few verses about that Bible person. But whether the Bible offers a little insight or a lot, there is much more to learn. With hints and suggestions about where to look and what to look for, the discovery method draws you further into the life and times of each Bible person introduced in this series. To help focus the discovery method, the three organizing questions for each session provide a direction for investigation.

The first question, What does the Bible say about the person? delves into the Scripture text for specific references about the Bible figure.

Some of the persons featured in this series are characters whose record in Scripture is quite brief, perhaps only a few verses. Others are much more prominent. When the biblical information is scant, you will be able to review all the references. If the Bible figure is more prominent, only a selection of representative passages are indicated. If you want to dig deeper, the Bible reference tools will help you locate more information.

Whether the biblical references are few or numerous, the Bible and other sources offer much more information than you might immediately notice.

The second question, What else would we like to know about the Bible person? mines the less direct sources of information.

What is the context of the action? Who are the related characters who the featured Bible person influenced or was influenced by? What are the social and economic conditions that help us understand the person and his or her situation? Where does the action take place? These and other questions expand the picture and help you see more fully into the life and times of each biblical character in these studies.

Once the portrait has become more clear, the third question, How does what I know about this person affect my life and faith? helps you apply your new insights to your own life.

This question is the "so what?" or the "now what?" aspect of the study that links the ancient text to our contemporary lives and issues. In answering this question, the study facilitates self-discovery and, we hope, spiritual growth and transformation.

Bible People and Study Skills

All learners have different levels of acquaintance with the Bible and of skills to study the Bible. This article presents a few pointers for how to approach *Bible People,* depending on the level of those skills. Refer to the list on the inside back cover for a description of each of the tools mentioned.

Beginning Skills

Use a study Bible

- Use a good study Bible with notes, cross-referencing, and maps. Buy a new one if you need to.
- Be sure that the text is a translation that is readable and understandable for you. *Bible People* uses the New Revised Standard Version as its primary translation.
- Take some time to learn how to "get around" in the Bible. Use the table of contents to find the books and to see what else is in there. Many Bibles have articles, charts, maps, and other information in addition to the biblical text.
- *Get Acquainted With The Bible* (Abingdon Press) is an excellent introductory resource to help you learn what is in the Bible and how to use it. (Call 1-800-672-1789 and order #140463.)

Look over a one-volume dictionary of the Bible.

- Check to see if it contains a table of contents and/or an index.
- Read any self-promotional material that will help you understand what is contained in the dictionary.
- Then thumb through it, randomly reading any entry that catches your eye.

Acquaint yourself with a Bible commentary, perhaps a one-volume commentary for starters.

- Choose three or four of your favorite Bible passages and look them up, noting what new insights come from an expanded view of the text.
- Peruse the table of contents to see what else is there and skim through the articles.

Intermediate Skills

Introduce yourself to the other study tools: concordance, atlas, other sources.

- Pick a key word from one of your favorite texts and look it up in the concordance. Is the same text in more than one passage? How is that key term used elsewhere?
- Look up a concept, such as *hospitality* or *marriage* in a topical concordance. What are the citations? How are these entries different from an alphabetical concordance?
- Check for a table of contents or an index, or flip through the pages to see what else is contained in the concordance. Read the introduction, if there is one.
- Thumb through an atlas to see what kinds of maps, graphs, charts, and other information is there.
- Look up the places mentioned from one of your favorite Bible stories. How far are they from each other? What is the terrain like? What would a traveler be likely to encounter on the route?
- Check to see if key information is provided for particular cities (like Jerusalem) or for prominent geographical features (such as Mount Horeb). If this is not in the atlas, use a Bible dictionary as well.

Read the text, then ask questions of the text.

- Who is involved in this passage? Who do they represent?
- Who is not present? Who is not represented?
- What is going on?
- Who is the audience? What are they like?
- Who is involved with the central figure(s) of the text? What impact do the characters have on each other?
- What is the context? What is the central message?
- What did that message mean then? What relevance does it have now? now for you?
- What is not happening?
- What emotions might have been felt by the figures presenting the story, text, or action? by the audience? now by you?
- What do you notice about the story, after using several resources to gain more information, that you didn't know or notice before? What difference does that make to your faith and understanding now?

Advanced Skills

Dig deeper into the cultural aspects and other details.

● Use the Bible study tools to look into details that the text suggests or assumes its original readers would already understand, such as, What did it mean to be a slave or widow or head of household? What did neighboring religions do in the same situation or region? Where is the action taking place and what was the situation there? How much is something worth? How long did it take to get there and what method of travel would have been used? What was the social/economic/political climate historically?

Use biblical-era sources in addition to the Bible and standard reference tools.

● Certain biblical passages are mentioned also in the Apocrypha or the historical context is the same. Check them out. Many Bibles include the Apocrypha, which most Orthodox religious groups (such as Roman Catholics) and some Protestant denominations (such as Episcopalians) regard as part of the canonized (or "official") Scripture.

● Look for references, concepts, and historical events in church encyclopedias, dictionaries, or historical writings. You may need an excellent public library or a theological library to obtain these texts, although most good bookstores have some biblical-era references.

Cross-reference passages to see what is said about the same or similar situation elsewhere in the Bible.

● When an annotated Bible provides cross-references or notes that refer to other passages, look them up.

● Many passages, especially in the Gospels, are recorded more than once. Look up the same event in another biblical book to see how it differs or agrees with the other citation(s).

● Ask yourself the exploratory questions as you compare texts.

● Use a concordance to look for several instances of the same word, event, social situation, and so on in the Bible. Look up the various references to see how the Bible's treatment varies (or not) to get a composite picture or overview of an issue.

Chapter One

Apollos

**CHOOSE FROM THE FOL-
LOWING ACTIVITIES TO
REFLECT ON APOLLOS AS
A FOLLOWER OF JESUS.**

Meet Apollos

 Invite the group to read Acts 18:24-28. Have them discuss the following and enter responses in the space provided.

 How would you describe the advice Priscilla and Aquila gave Apollo? Why do you suppose Apollo needed it? What new place was he encouraged to minister? Why do you suppose he was in need of encouragement? Why was it important for the disciples, who were in the location to which Apollos was going, to welcome him?

 Have the group read 1 Corinthians 3:5-9. Invite them to answer: How did Paul identify Apollos? How would you connect Paul's words to your understanding of the word *disciple?* Was Apollo identified as a disciple? Why?

What Does the Bible Say About Apollos?

Meet Apollos

Apollos was a Jewish convert from Alexandria, Egypt. He became a follower of Jesus after following John the Baptist. Apollos came to Ephesus, located in Asia Minor. While there, he showed that he knew the Scriptures well and taught accurately the things concerning Jesus. Also in Ephesus, Priscilla and Aquila, who were friends of the apostle Paul, gave Apollos some important information of use to him in his ministry. The believers in Ephesus encouraged him in his desire to go to a southern province in Greece to minister. They wrote the disciples to welcome him there (Acts 18:24-28).

The advice given by Priscilla and Aquila:

The name of the Southern Province:

In 1 Corinthians 3:5-9, Paul calls attention to Apollos' leadership by referring to him in relation to God:

Ask group members to recall three places where Apollos carried out his ministry. Invite them to find the places on a map. Identify the places.

Have the group identify key words describing Apollos based on what they have read.

Have them summarize in short sentences who Apollo was? As these sentences are given, put them on the board or on newsprint.

Expand Your Knowledge

Read Acts 18:24-28, with emphasis on Apollos' ministry roles and personal qualities/attitudes. Since the Scripture is short, have the entire group read it aloud. Or divide the group in half with each half reading alternate verses.

Paul's specific words:

In his letter to Titus (3:13), Paul urged Apollos to revisit a particular church and instructed Titus to help Apollos on his way there:

The church to revisit:

What Else Would We Like to Know About Apollos?

We discover more about Apollos in Acts 18:24-19:1 and 1 Corinthians 1:10-4:1-6.

Expand Your Knowledge

In Acts 18:24-28, we discover that Apollos carried out at least four ministry roles including learner, speaker, teacher, and helper. In carrying out these roles, he also displayed personal qualities and attitudes that were complimentary to what he was doing as a follower of Jesus:

Ask participants to write the qualities/attitudes in the space provided. Have them discuss the importance of the ministry roles and the qualities/attitudes to being a follower of Jesus.

Ministry	Personal Qualities/Attitudes	Roles
Learner		
Speaker		
Teacher		
Helper		

Ministry		Importance of Role
Learner		
Speaker		
Teacher		
Helper		

Leadership in the Diverse Corinthian Church

 Ask group members, either individually or divided into small groups to use a Bible commentary or reference tool to carry out the suggestions below. Have them record their responses in the spaces provided, and report findings to the main group:

Explore the nature and origin of Apollos's viewpoint.

 Compare Apollos's views with Paul's and Cephas's views.

Servanthood in the Diverse Corinthian Church

Apollos's ministry in Corinth took place within the decade beginning A.D. 50. This period was a time when Corinth's intellectual life and commercial possibilities attracted people of many cultural backgrounds. A thriving Jewish community lived there. Gentiles lived there. Temples dedicated to Greek, Egyptian, and Eastern gods showed that a large pagan population from various cultures lived there.

Many Corinthian inhabitants apparently came from humble or slave backgrounds (1 Corinthians 1:26). Corinth held potential for them to build a better life than they had known before. Competition among the various groups thrived. Competitive attitudes shaped by differing points of view about the Christian way caused divisions in the Christian community. Exclusive groups formed out of people's awareness of the differing points of view of church leaders about the Christian way. Apollos and Cephas, also known as Peter, were among the leaders. Apollos's perspective differed from Cephas's views. The views of both Apollos and Cephas differed from Paul's perspective. The following Scripture in Paul's Letter to the Corinthians tells us about the controversial and divisive issue in the Christian community. This letter suggests, for our consideration, Apollos's view and the impact diverse viewpoints had on the Christian community.

Discover the impact of Apollos's views on others.

Dramatize the Corinthian church situation. Or organize a debate team with a representative for each view. Have each one defend their view before the large group. Give each a chance for rebuttal. Ask remaining group members to take sides and tell why. Discuss the impact of the drama.

Read 1 Corinthians 1:10—3:1-9

Apollos's view:

Comparison of Apollos's view with the views of Paul and Cephas:

Impact of Apollos's view on the community:

Diversity Today

Have the group brainstorm all of the ways Christians differ today culturally, experientially, and in terms of Christian living. Put the responses on a chalk or marker board or a large piece of paper. Discuss where and why differences cause conflict and division.

Invite the group to discover what the following Scriptures say about belonging, success, servanthood with a purpose, ministry team work, and receiving care as they apply to Apollos:

Diversity Today

As in Apollos's time, the Christian Church today includes people from diverse cultural backgrounds. People differ in what they seek from and contribute to the church. They differ in their expression of beliefs, values, and approaches to living the Christian way in everyday life. As with Apollos, people live out their lives as Jesus' followers with good intentions. How they do it impacts the lives of others. Paul's words about the situation in which Apollos participated were to stimulate the members to consider carefully what was needed to mend the division.

♦ 1 Corinthians 1:10-17; 3:1-9

♦ 1 Corinthians 3:1-9

♦ Titus 3:13

 Discuss what each term means today.

 Explore why each term was important in Apollos's time and is important today.

 Examine ways people today might interfere with the positive attainment of the terms.

 Suggest ways to prevent or address actions that might block the positive attainment of belonging, success, servanthood with a purpose, servanthood through team effort, and receiving care.

 Use the terms to make large posters or banners to display in your meeting place or church.

Collect magazine pictures or family pictures from members to make a collage of diversity. Include the terms discussed in the collage.

Belonging

The Corinthian church found in Paul's letter several questions related to belonging. These questions appear in 1 Corinthians 1:10- 17 and 3:1-9. Based on what we read there, we may consider what meaning Paul assigned to the word *belonging* and what *belonging* means in our churches today.

Explore in the whole group or in small groups the questions:

- Where has God called (or is calling) you to intentionally live the Christian way?

- Through what roles, personal qualities/attitudes do you carry out the Christian way in your home, church, and community?

Have them jot down their thoughts in the space provided.

What Are My Views?

Have group members choose a partner. Invite them to explore with their partner their views of living the Christian way in light of what they know about the views of Apollos, Cephas, and Paul.

After the partners share, invite responses in the large group. You may ask the following:
What did you learn about yourself? What did you learn from your partner that helped you to think about your own views? Would you now change any of your views? Why or why not?

Apollos As Successful Servant

Apollos' personal qualities and attitudes were attributes that contributed to his ministry as servant (Acts 18:24-28). The Corinthian church found in Paul's letter a statement about the source of his success. We find this statement in 1 Corinthians 3:1-9.

The statement:

Apollos as Servant With a Purpose

Apollos carried out his servanthood in specific ways (Acts 18:24-28). The Corinthian church found the purpose and the outcome of servanthood in 1 Corinthians 3:1-9.

Purpose of servanthood:

outcome of servanthood:

Apollos As Ministry Team Member

Priscilla and Aquila made a special point of making Apollos aware of what it means to live the Christian way in community (Acts 18:24-28). The Corinthian church found in Paul's letter the expected relationship of Apollos to Paul and to the members (1 Corinthians 3:1-9).

The expected relationship:

Apollos as Recipient of Care

Disciples need encouragement and help along the way. The believers encouraged Apollos to continue in ministry where he was needed (Acts 18:24-28). Titus received word from Paul regarding the extent of care he was to give Apollos. We find this request of Paul in Titus 3:13.

The extent of care requested:

How Does What I Now Know About Apollos Affect My Life and Faith?

Where and How Do I Serve?
Apollos sought to live the Christian way and to do what he could to bring about the conversion of others to this way. He did this in several locations. Consider places in your everyday life where you feel God wants you to live and show others the Christian way.

Through recounting Apollos's personal attitudes and qualities as a disciple, consider your present attitudes and qualities as a Christian, ones you would like to develop, and how you might develop them.

What Are My Views?
Apollos had a particular perspective on what the Christian way is all about. Assess your views in light of what you know about the views of Apollos, Paul, and Cephas, and consider the impact of your views on others.

How Do I Deal With Diversity?

 Organize teams of two or three persons. Have the teams develop concrete strategies for dealing with conflict resulting from diverse cultures and views.

 Have the teams share their strategies with the whole group.

Discuss the pros and cons of implementing the strategies in light of our understanding of belonging, success, servanthood with a purpose, ministry team work, and receiving care.

In Closing

 Have the group review lesson highlights. Then discuss the questions listed on the opposite side.

 Invite the group to read silently the words to the song, "Weave." Ask them to comment on the connection of the words to the group's application of their study of Apollo to our journey as followers of Jesus today. Close by learning and singing the song.

How Do I Deal With Diversity?

Belonging, success, purpose, outcome of discipleship, team work, and care-receiving are themes appearing in Scriptures that refer to Apollos. Consider meanings of these themes in situation(s) of diversity and conflict about which you are aware and ways of applying the themes to end conflict.

Chapter Two

John

CHOOSE FROM THE FOLLOWING ACTIVITIES TO REFLECT ON JOHN AS A DISCIPLE AND YOUR OWN JOURNEY AS A DISCIPLE

Meet John

 Have different groups read Matthew 4:18-22; Mark 1:16-20; and Luke 5:1-11.

 Invite the groups to compare the three accounts of John's call to discipleship.

 Have the groups to review silently their memory of the story.

 Invite group members to study the map for the location. Then enact the story of John's call with attention to the setting, characters, and key words.

 Discuss in small groups insights from the enactment.

What Does the Bible Say About John?

Meet John

When Jesus called the first disciples, John was among them (Matthew 4:18-22; Mark 1:16-20; Luke 5:1-11). Jesus later appointed him as one of the Twelve, whom he also named apostles (Mark 3:13-19). John grew up in a family of fishermen in the Lake Gennesaret region along with his brother James, who was also called and named an apostle. They embarked upon a new life in response to Jesus' invitation. Entering the new life as a disciple meant that John and his brother had to leave their father Zebedee and the family's livelihood to follow Jesus as fishers of people.

Of all the founding apostles, John, along with Peter and James, formed a circle of close associates of Jesus. Within that circle, John witnessed many things, undertook other specific roles as a close associate of Jesus, and carried out a distinctive ministry as an apostle.

John as Witness

 Have individuals read silently or aloud Scriptures shown in the main text about John as witness.

 Instruct group members to jot down what John witnessed, where and with whom in the space provided. Discuss what witness means and its importance to John's discipleship.

John as Witness

We learn what John witnessed as Jesus' follower in several Scriptures:

Scripture	What	Where	With Whom	What Was Witnessed
Mark 5:21-43 or Luke 8:40-56				
Matthew 17:1-13 or Mark 9:2-13 or Luke 9:28-36				
Acts 1:1-14				

John as Jesus' Helper

John as Jesus' Helper

 Have individuals read silently or aloud Scriptures shown in the main text about John as Jesus' helper.

 Instruct group members to jot down helper roles, where and with whom they were enacted in the space provided. Invite discussion about what helping means in discipleship.

We discover other actions John took as a close associate and helper of Jesus in the following Scriptures:

Scripture	Roles	Where	With Whom
Matthew 26:36-46 or Mark 14:32-42			
Luke 22:7-13			

John's Ministry as Apostle

John's Ministry as Apostle

 Have individuals read silently or aloud Scriptures shown in the main text about John's ministry as an apostle.

 Instruct group members to jot down John's ministry functions, where and with whom he carried them out in the space provided. Discuss the meaning of the word *apostle* and how it differs from the word *disciple*.

We uncover the nature of John's apostolic functions in the following Scriptures:

Scripture	Roles	Where	With Whom
Acts 3:1-23			
Acts 8:14-17			
Acts 8:25			
Galatians 2:9-10			

Build on Your Knowledge About John

 Invite the group to name specific family members present during John's call.

Build on Your Knowledge About John

We already know that John grew up in a family of fishermen. We also know that he had a brother named James, who was also called to be Jesus' disciple and was sent to be an apostle. And we know that their father's name was Zebedee. But, so far, their mother's identity remains a mystery as well as other aspects of John's identity.

The Mystery of John's Mother

 Divide the group in half. Have the groups read verses from Matthew 27:45-55 alternately. Have them jot down who John's mother was in the space provided.

 Invite the groups to explore why John's mother might not have been mentioned earlier and how they feel about it.

The Mystery of John's Mother

The account of Jesus' death and those who witnessed it (Matthew 27:45-56) gives us some insight about who John's mother was.

The Mystery of the Beloved Disciple

 Have group members read silently John 13:23-25, 19:25-27, 20:2-10, 21:7, and 21:20-23.

 Have group members divide a sheet of paper in half. On one half, list all reasons for believing John was the

The Mystery of the Beloved Disciple

Some scholars refer to John as the "beloved disciple" based on what is written in the Gospel of John 13:23-25; 19:25-27; 20:2-10; 21:7; and 21:20-23. Others dispute that this is true, based on the fact that John is not specifically identified in the Scriptures. We find clues that help us address the dispute in John 21:24, and in our identifying the person

"beloved disciple." On the other half, list all reasons for believing he was not the "beloved disciple."

Have the whole group read together John 21:24. Then have each participant jot down clues to who the "beloved disciple" is based on the Scripture.

with whom the beloved disciple appears in almost every instance.

Clues to who the "beloved disciple" is:

What Else Would We Like to Know About John?

What Else Would We Like to Know About John?

John's Special Request

 Divide into two groups. Ask one group to read Matthew 20:20-28 and record the request, Jesus' response to it, and the impact the request had on the disciples in the space provided. Also ask them to be ready to role-play the story account. Ask the other group to read Mark 10:35-40 and follow the directions given to the first group.

 Have the two groups share their responses and present the role-plays. Invite discussion about the differences between the two accounts and how they felt about the request.

John's Special Request

Either John, along with his brother, or their mother, made a special request to Jesus. They really wanted Jesus to honor the request. What was it? We learn of this request, Jesus' response to it, and the impact this request had on other disciples in Matthew 20:20-23 and Mark 10:35-40.

The request:

Jesus' response to the request:

Impact this request had on the other disciples:

Invite the group to compare John's special request to the Luke 23:39-43 account of the request made by one of the criminals who was hanged beside Jesus. Also compare Jesus' response to John's special request and the one made by the criminal. Have the group discuss their feelings about this scenario compared to their feelings about John's special request.

John's Commitment

 Have participants explore the extent of John's commitment by reading silently Acts 4:1-22. Write in the space provided the basis for John's persecution, the form it took and his attitudes. Reflect on meanings of commitment then and now.

John's Commitment

John was with Peter in some important missions. These fellow missionaries had to be committed and maintain a particular attitudinal frame of mind to carry out their ministry. Doing so was important because, as shown in Acts 4:1-22, they had to withstand persecution. We discover in this Scripture the basis for their persecution, the form it took, and the attitudinal frame of mind John and his fellow missionaries held on to.

Basis for persecution:

Form the persecution took:

Attitude of John and his fellow missionaries:

The Cost of Following Jesus

 Ask different subgroups to find what happened to Peter, James, and John in Acts 12:1-19 and Revelation 1:9. Discuss the cost of discipleship then and now.

The Cost of Following Jesus

We might expect that the close relationship between Peter, James, and John would continue to appear in Scripture. But this is not the case. All was not easy for these followers of Jesus. We will discover what happened to John's brother James in Acts 12:1-2.

In Acts 12:3-19, we discover a chain of events that center on Peter, John's longtime fellow apostle.

In Revelation 1:9, John says that he was on the isle of Patmos. Christian tradition says that he got there through the actions of the Roman authorities. We will find in a Bible dictionary, Bible commentary, or other Bible reference books more about what and where Patmos was and why John was there.

John the Author and Elder

 Have participants discover how John refers to himself in the salutations of his First and Second Letters. Find in a Bible dictionary the roles of elders and discuss how John fulfills these roles through his letters.

 Encourage group members to read the letters and the Book

John the Author and Elder

John is considered by some Bible scholars to be the author of the three epistles that carry his name as well as the Book of Revelation. The salutations in at least two of the epistles point to John's age/stage at the time he wrote them.

The Book of Revelation suggests that John probably wrote the book while on

of Revelation on their own, using Bible reference materials.

Patmos. We learn about the purposes, the situation, and the themes found in John's writing by reading the short epistles and Revelation as well as Bible commentaries on them.

Purposes:

Situations:

Themes:

Called to Discipleship and Apostleship Today

 Have group members reflect on people's special requests, commitments, costs, and responsibilities that accompany discipleship today. Jot down ideas in the space provided.

Called to Discipleship and Apostleship Today

Like John, many people today freely choose to follow Jesus. These disciples accept a mission by seeing themselves in Christian vocation. Some heed a call by God to apostolic leadership. They are commissioned to preach the gospel and serve God's people as ordained clergy. Consider what kinds of special requests, commitment, costs, and other responsibilities accompany discipleship and apostleship today.

Special requests:

Commitment:

Costs:

Responsibilities:

How Does What I Now Know About John Affect My Life and Faith?

What Does it Mean for Me to Be Called?

 Invite group members to make journal entries.

Ask the group to enter into a silent summation of the account of John's call to be a disciple and an apostle.

Ask members to form a mental picture of what the call to discipleship and apostleship is like today. Who calls? To whom is the call made? Where does the call happen?

Ask them to reflect and then write on where, when, and how they have experienced the call to follow Jesus.

Invite members to enter into a silent summation of the accounts of John as witness, Jesus' helper, and as an apostle. Then write those roles and functions in which they now enact and any ones that were triggered by John's.

What Does it Mean for Me to Be Called?

By following Jesus, John accepted a new life priority. Re-read the event of John's call in Matthew 4:18-22, Mark 1:16-20, and Luke 5:1-11. Consider where, when, and how you have experienced the call to follow Jesus.

Recall instances that showed John as a witness, Jesus' helper, and apostle. Examine how these actions might apply to your life. Recall any experiences you have had of witnessing or helping and any call you have had to be an apostle.

Reflect on meanings John's special request to Jesus has for your life during youth, adulthood, and elderhood. Examine whether the words of the hymn, "Are Ye Able," apply to you (*The United Methodist Hymnal*, 530).

Have members read the words to the song, "Are Ye Able" (*The United Methodist Hymnal*, 530). Then have them write a response to the question in their own words. The response may be in the form of a poem, prayer, or short story.

Recall what commitment and cost meant to John. Examine what Christian discipleship is worth to you. Consider any conditions beyond which you would not go as a follower of Jesus.

In Closing

 Invite the group to use the questions found in the main text to reflect openly on the group's deliberations.

In the spirit of prayer, focus on what you (the students) personally gained from this study and how you would live out your life as a disciple of Christ. End with a short prayer.

In Closing

What meanings did this lesson hold for you? What insights or learning did you gain? What surprised you? What assumptions or beliefs were challenged and reinforced? In what ways did you experience God as you moved through the lesson and learned about John?

Chapter Three

Mary Magdalene

CHOOSE FROM THE FOL-
LOWING ACTIVITIES TO
REFLECT ON MARY MAG-
DALENE AS CHRISTIAN
LEADER.

Meet Mary Magdalene

 Invite group members to share what they may already know about Mary Magdalene. Have them read silently the opening information about Mary Magdalene in the main text. Ask them to identify key words that characterize her and list them on a large piece of paper. Then have them give preliminary thoughts on which words reflect their understanding of a disciple and why.

 Find a map in a Bible dictionary and find the name of Mary Magdalene's hometown.

What Does the Bible Say About Mary Magdalene?

Meet Mary Magdalene

Mary Magdalene, or Mary of Magdala, is regarded as an important leader among a group of women who followed and served Jesus. The women remained steadfast followers from the very beginning of Jesus' ministry in Galilee to his death on Golgotha, and thereafter. Nothing is known about the family of Mary Magdalene. Her name probably derives from the town called Magdala, located on Lake Gennesaret. We will recall from Chapter 2 (of the previous study) that John the apostle came from the Lake Gennesaret region. We will find Magdala on the west shore between Gennesaret and Tiberias.

A Question About Who Mary Was or Was Not

 Ask the group to read silently or divide the group in half, each group reading alternate verses of Luke 7:36-50. Then have them jot down in the spaces provided their recall of how the woman was introduced and what she did. If they read silently, have someone recount it in their own words.

 Have group members use a Bible dictionary, Bible commentary on the Gospel of Luke, and other Bible interpretation resources to discover additional information about the woman and her sin. Invite them to jot down their findings in the space provided and share them with the group.

 Ask the group to read aloud John 12:1-8. Then jot down in the spaces provided their memory of how the women were introduced and what one woman did that is akin to the woman's act in Luke 7:37-38.

 Use a Bible dictionary, Bible commentary on the Gospel of John, or other interpretation resources to discover additional information about the two women and their relationship to each other. Have group members share

A Question About Who Mary Magdalene Was or Was Not

From about the sixth century, the Western church accepted that Mary Magdalene was the sinner whose life changed when she went to see Jesus at Simon the Pharisee's house (Luke 7:36-50). However, the Eastern church rejected this notion. Bible scholars today also question this notion since Luke does not name her. We may discover some of the problem about who she was or was not. We do this by exploring, first, how Luke 7:36-50 presents the woman and, then, by comparing what we find with other relevant Scriptures.

How the woman in Luke 7:36-50 is introduced:

What the woman did:

What we know about her identity:

In John 12:1-8, two women are introduced and their actions are described. Both are presented differently from the one in Luke's account. However, one of them does something akin to what the woman did as told in Luke 7:37-38. We may also note in the Gospel of John the probable relationship of the two women to each other. How they are identified

the information. Then compare what they found with what they know of the woman in Luke 7:36-50.

 Ask group members to read aloud Luke 8:1-3. Then have them jot down in the spaces provided their memory of the women's names and what they were doing.

 Use a commentary on Luke, Bible dictionary, or other resources to discover additional information about the three women. Share the information. Have the group compare this information with what they know of the woman in Luke 7:36-50.

 Raise the four questions appearing in the main text for discussion.

 Invite them to decide on and discuss arguments helpful to arriving at a conclusion about whether Mary Magdalene was the woman in Luke 7:36-50. Help them by asking added questions:
- With which tradition do you agree: The Western church tradition or the Eastern church tradition?
- Why do you think there was a problem in determining whether Mary Magdalene was the sinner woman?
- What Scripture and other sources gave you the most helpful information with which to draw a conclusion?

and their relationship to each other informs us whether or not one is Mary from Magdala.

How the women in John 12:1-8 are introduced:

What one woman did that is akin to what we find in Luke 7:37-38:

What we conclude about the women's identities in comparison to the woman in Luke 7:36-50:

Three women are introduced in Luke 8:1-3. The Scripture introduces all three by name. The passage also tells what they were doing and that all three experienced a life-changing event as did the woman in Luke 7:36-50.

The names by which the women in Luke 8:1-3 are introduced:

What the women were doing:

Finally, we may draw some conclusions about whether the woman in Luke 8:2 is the same woman as the one in Luke 7:36-50 by comparing Luke 7:37, 48, 50 to Luke 8:2 and Mark 16:9. We might also consider the following:

1. Why would Luke carefully name Mary Magdalene in Luke 8:2 and not do so in Luke 7:36-50 if he knew the sinful woman was she?
2. Is the woman's sin and experience of forgiveness of sin and salvation by faith the same as Mary Magdalene's evil spirits and infirmities and their cure?
3. Should the other women named in Luke 7:37 be just as suspect as Mary Magdalene since they, too, were cured of evil spirits and infirmities?
4. What other questions might we raise and seek answers? What is our final conclusion?

Mary Magdalene as Jesus' Follower and Provider

 Have group members discover definitions of the words *follow* and *provide* in a dictionary of New Testament words or Bible dictionary.

 Have the group compare Mary Magdalene's roles of follower and provider with the roles of the twelve disciples and the way they entered their roles. Do this by first asking all group members to read silently the Scriptures indicated in the main text and complete the exercises as indicated. Then invite them to review Luke 8:1-3, Mark 15:40-41, and Matthew 27:55-56. Engage the group in discussion of the differences.

Mary Magdalene as Jesus' Follower and Provider

We have already found in Luke 8:1-3 that Mary Magdalene accompanied and provided for Jesus as he went from city to city and village to village bringing the good news of God's reign. She, the other women, and the twelve disciples were with Jesus.

In Mark 15:40-41; and Matthew 27:55-56, the word "follower" describes Mary Magdalene's relationship with Jesus throughout his ministry. This word also reflects what is said about the Twelve. However, the identification of Mary's role as "provider" in Luke 8:3 and Matthew 27:55-56 is unique. Being a provider meant that she prepared for the practical needs of Jesus' itinerating mission. She presented to him financial support for this mission. There is no indication that she was sought out to fulfill this role. In this way, her role of provider contrasts with the roles of the twelve disciples and the way they entered their roles. We become aware of the differences as we explore the following Scriptures:

Scriptures	How the Disciples Entered	Their Roles
Mark 1:20; 13:13; Luke 6:13		
Mark 13:14a		
Mark 13:14b		
Mark 13:14c-15		
Luke 10:1-3		

What Else Do We Want to Know About Mary Magdalene?

 Have group members read silently or aloud in small groups the Gospel passages indicated in each of the sections below. After each section, have them complete the exercises in spaces provided. If you form small groups, the various Scriptures can be divided among them. Look for the sections in the main text called: "The Gospels Tell About Mary Magdalene at the Crucifixion"; "The Gospels Tell About Mary Magdalene at

What Else Do We Want to Know About Mary Magdalene?

Mary Magdalene's role as a follower of Jesus was not short-lived. She was a steadfast follower. She came with Jesus when he made an appeal to the nation in Jerusalem (Mark 15:41). She was at Jesus' crucifixion (Mark 15:40; Luke 23:55; Matthew 27:55-56; and John 19:25). She was at Jesus' burial (Mark 15:47; Luke 23:55-56; and Matthew 27:61). And she was at Jesus' resurrection (Mark 16:1-9; Luke 24:1-12; Matthew 28:1-10; and John 20:1-18).

Jesus' Burial"; and "The Gospels Tell About Mary Magdalene at Jesus' Resurrection."

In reading about Mary Magdalene's journey with Jesus in the four Gospels, we should keep in mind that the Gospel of Mark was likely the earliest account. For this reason, we consider it our primary source of information. Moreover, scholars believe that the probable chronological order of the Gospels is Mark, Luke, Matthew, and John. This means that we will look at what the Gospel writers had to say about Mary Magdalene in that order.

The Gospels tell about Mary Magdalene at the Crucifixion

Scripture	What it Says About Mary Magdalene
Mark 15:40	
Luke 23:55	
Matthew 27:55-56	
John 19:25	

The Gospels Tell About Mary Magdalene at Jesus' Burial

Scripture   *What it Says About Mary Magdalene*

Mark 15:47

Luke 23:55-56

Matthew 27:61

The Gospels Tell About Mary Magdalene at Jesus' Resurrection

Scripture   *What it Says About Mary Magdalene*

Mark 16:1-9

Luke 24:1-12, with
emphasis on
verses 10-12.

Luke 24:13-24, with
emphasis on
verses 22-24.

Matthew 28:1-10

John 20:1-18

Mary Magdalene as Leader of Women in Jesus' Day

 Ask group members to recall aloud or jot down in the space provided who Mary Magdalene was, how she was presented in the various Scriptures, and the roles she carried out.

Mary Magdalene as Leader of Women in Jesus' Day

Critics of the roles of women in Scripture say that Mary Magdalene, as others, performed subservient and peripheral roles. We may draw our own conclusions about whether this was the case with Mary Magdalene. We do this by recalling who

Invite them to think about the most striking thing they learned about Mary Magdalene as leader and why. Have group members compare thoughts with one or two other persons.

she was, how she was presented in Scripture, and the roles she carried out.

Regardless of our conclusion, we find in the four Gospels a woman whose name appears in many places. We also find a woman whose devotion as Jesus' follower and provider is recounted time and time again.

How Does What I Know About Mary Magdalene Affect My Life and Faith?

Deciding to Follow Jesus

Invite group members either to make journal entries, or to have a discussion by doing the following:

● Invite them to reflect on when, where, and why they decided to follow Jesus and where they are in their journey now.

After making journal entries, invite open discussion.

Deciding to Follow Jesus
People become followers of Jesus in a variety of ways. Some grow up in the church. They regard their joining a church their formal commitment to what has always been. Others respond to a feeling of being "strangely warm," or a nudge to commit their lives to Christ. Still others experience life-changing events, similar to Mary Magdalene's, that set them on a journey of devoted Christian service. Knowing Mary Magdalene's story offers us opportunity to reflect on when, where, and why we decided to follow Jesus and/or where we are in our journey now.

Providing for Christian Mission

Invite individuals to continue making journal entries or to continue discussing by doing the following:

Providing for Christian Mission
Mary Magdalene's devoted service to Jesus included providing for his itinerant mission by preparing for the journey. Her service also included supporting the mission financially. Knowing the nature of

- Invite them to reflect on how they have prepared, or are preparing, to live as Christians.
- Invite them to reflect on past and present contributions to others' preparation for Christian living and service.

 After making journal entries, invite open discussion.

Steadfastness in Service

 Invite individuals to continue making journal entries or to continue discussing by doing the following:

- Invite them to reflect on how they show loyalty to Jesus Christ.
- Ask them to consider how their study of Mary Magdalene may contribute to their ongoing loyalty.
- Invite them to reflect on personal meanings they assign to the words of the songs mentioned. The group may wish to sing the songs.

Leaders of Women Today

 Ask group members to name any women today who have carried out a ministry similar to Mary Magdalene's ministry. Ask them also if they regard these women as leaders and why.

Raise questions for discussion: Who is a Christian leader? What are the qualities of Christian leadership?

Mary Magdalene's role as provider offers us opportunity to consider how we prepare ourselves to live as Christians. This knowledge also offers us opportunity to consider what we contribute to others' preparation and to Christ's mission where we are and beyond.

Steadfastness in Service

Mary Magdalene remained a loyal follower of Jesus, including during difficult times. Our knowledge of her steadfastness gives us opportunity to consider the nature and extent of our loyalty to Jesus Christ. We may meditate on the songs "Where He Leads Me" and "I Surrender All" *(The United Methodist Hymnal,* 338 and 354).

Leaders of Women Today

Over the years, women have continued to carry out significant leadership roles wherever needed in church and society based on their devotion to Jesus. The roles of women devotees continues today. At the same time, critics comment about the roles of women who are followers of Jesus today in ways similar to comments about Mary Magdalene's roles. Our awareness of this matter offers us

Who is a provider for Christian mission? What are the qualities of providers?

 Organize a "fishbowl" in which three to four women volunteer to be in the center of a circular seating arrangement. Tell them they are to represent "The Mary Magdalene Christian Mission Circle." They are to make position statements on the following:
- the varieties of roles in which women of all adult ages/stages are needed today to carry out the ministry of Jesus Christ;
- the preparation they need to carry it out; and
- the kinds of support they need to maintain steadfast service.

In Closing

 Explore individually or in small groups the questions appearing in the main text. Then have small groups write a prayer of gratitude for the ministry of Mary Magdalene and for illumination of where God is working to bring women into Christian leadership today. Have each group choose one to read their prayer. After each prayer, ask all to respond with "Hear our prayer, O God" and "Amen" at the end.

opportunity to reflect on present and potential roles of Christian women today. Our awareness also offers us opportunity to reflect on what the angel's call to Mary Magdalene to tell others about the risen Christ means for all of us today.

What meanings did this lesson hold for you? What insights or learning did you gain? What surprised you? What assumptions or beliefs were challenged and reinforced? In what ways did you experience God as you moved through the lesson and learned about Mary Magdalene?

Chapter Four

Mary and Martha

Meet Mary and Martha

Before asking the group to turn to the chapter on Mary and Martha, ask them to focus on the map on which they located the homes of John the apostle and Mary Magdalene. Ask them to imagine themselves traveling south from Galilee to Samaria and continuing South toward Judea. Tell them that they will stop at Jerusalem and then continue two miles east to Bethany where sisters named Mary and Martha lived.

As they imagine traveling to Bethany, tell them the current name of the village. Introduce Mary and Martha, using opening statements about them found in the text.

What Does the Bible Say About Mary and Martha?

Meet Mary and Martha

Mary and Martha were sisters from Bethany, a village about two miles east of Jerusalem. Their brother Lazarus also lived there. This village was south of the homes of John the apostle and Mary Magdalene. The current name of the village is El-Azarieh, which is Arabic for Lazarion. The village received this name in the fourth century after a new village was built over the tomb of Lazarus.

Martha was the older sister and presumably the head of the household. Mary, Martha, and Lazarus were friends of Jesus. Mary and Martha made contact with Jesus when he came to Bethany. They also called for him during a troubling time in their lives.

Mary and Martha in the Gospel of Luke

 Have group members to look at some key messages Luke gets across before telling the sisters' story.
Read aloud Luke 3:6; 4:18-21; and 4:43. Sum up the message.
Read silently Luke 8:4-8, 11-15, 16-18, and 20-21. Have volunteers read aloud final comments found in Luke 8:8b, 15, 18, and 21. Follow up by asking the group members to write their comments. Also have them underline key words common to every comment.

Mary and Martha in the Gospel of Luke

One of the stories about Mary and Martha appears in the Gospel of Luke. This Gospel was written mainly for Gentiles and was perhaps influenced by the Roman court circle. Key messages in this account give us a foundation for considering the only story in the four Gospels of Jesus' visit to the sisters' home. One message shows Jesus' concern for all people. It characterizes Jesus' reaching out to people as the bearer of God's saving activity in Luke 3:6; 4:18-21; and 4:43. Luke also includes messages about an important requirement for followers of Jesus. We find it in:

Luke 8:8b as the final comment to verses 4-7

Luke 8:15 as the final comment to verses 11-14

Luke 8:18 as the final comment to verses 16-17

Luke 8:21 as the final comment to verses 19-20

**Setting Priorities
to Welcome Jesus**

Place on a large piece of paper or a board "A Frame work for Storytelling." Include sections called: The Setting, Occasion, Characters, Scenes including Actions and Dialogue in Them, Issue(s), and the Message(s). Then say aloud the framework sections.

 Invite the group to read Luke 10:38-42 silently. Have group members fill in aloud the storytelling framework.

 Have members to dramatize the story.

● Invite the group to explore various sides of the issue in the story and why they described the key message as they did.

● Invite the group into a word study. Provide English language dictionaries and a Bible dictionary or dictionary of New Testament words. Have members find and share with the group definitions and synonyms of the words *distraction, welcome,* and *receive.* Then have the group jot down in the space provided definitions and synonyms for the word *distraction.*

Setting Priorities To Welcome Jesus

In Luke 10:38-42, Martha welcomes Jesus into her home. As the story progresses, we discover that both Mary and Martha welcome him. But each receives him in a different way. We discover what happens and what it means by looking at the story setting, the occasion, the story characters, the story scenes including actions and dialogue in them, the issue in the story, and the key message:

The Scripture suggests that things Martha gave priority to became distractions. This assessment raises key questions for us to ponder. What does the word *distraction* mean? What specific things might have caused Martha's distraction? How do we understand the words *distraction, welcome,* and *receive* in light of Luke 4:18-19? How do we understand *distraction, welcome,* and *receive* in light of the final comments in Luke 8:8b, 15, 18, 21?

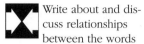

Write about and discuss relationships between the words *welcome* and *receive.*

Discuss chores, duties, and expectations that might have caused Martha's distraction.

Discuss the definitions of the words *distraction, welcome,* and *receive* in the story in light of Luke 4:18-19.

Talk about the definitions of the words *distraction, welcome,* and *receive* in light of the final comments in Luke 8:8b, 15, 18, 21.

Martha and Mary in the Gospel of John

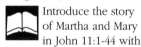

Introduce the story of Martha and Mary in John 11:1-44 with information about its location in the Gospel. Highlight the emphasis in the section where the story appears, using information from the text.

Martha and Mary in the Gospel of John

The Gospel of John presents the story of Martha and Mary in a situation involving their brother Lazarus' illness and death. The story is in the second major section of the Gospel. This section, covering John 2:1-12:20, emphasizes what Jesus revealed to the world through his public ministry. This section is often called "The Book of Signs" because of the seven signs appearing in it. The signs point to who Jesus is and the nature of his mission. This section also points to the kind of mature faith Jesus' followers should demonstrate. The story of Martha and Mary involves the seventh sign. We find it in John 11:1-44.

Examining Faith in Crisis

Have the group read the story in John 11:1-44 silently. Then recall the story using the storytelling framework.

Invite group members to compare the sisters' roles to the ones in Luke 10:38-42.

Ask volunteers to role play each sister's response to Jesus in John 11:21, 32. Include a role play of Jesus' response to them.

Discuss the impact of Jesus' response to each sister on the story direction.

● Have the group read aloud Martha's confession of faith in John 11:27. Use a commentary of John's Gospel or other Bible interpretation guides to explore meanings of the confession. Use small groups if there are several guides. Have them report findings to everyone.

● Compare Martha's confession with Peter's in Matthew 16:15-16. Discuss the importance of confessions of faith for disciples.

● Have small groups do the following after choosing group guide, recorder, and reporter:

Share learnings about who Jesus is and his mission from the story of Martha and Mary in John 11. Also share

Examining Faith in Crisis

As in Luke's story of the two sisters, the story in John's Gospel places them in different roles. By reading the story, we discover the situation in which their unique roles unfold.

We also discover in the story that both sisters trusted in Jesus; and they had faith in his healing power. They responded with identical words after Jesus failed to show up to heal Lazarus and arrived, instead, four days after he died. But Jesus' response to each of them differed.

John's Gospel does not tell us why Jesus responded to each of the sisters differently. Clearly he challenged Martha. She had to consider more depthfully who he really was and what her faith stance should have been within a broadened understanding of life and death (John 11:23-26). Martha rose to the challenge and confessed her faith in John 11:27. She does so in a manner reminiscent of Simon Peter's confession of faith in Matthew 16:15-16.

The seventh sign in John's Gospel is contained in John 11:38-44. Note what the sign is and at what point in the story it occurs. Note also that this sign occurs well after Martha's confession of faith. Recognition of these factors raises some

learnings about what mature faith means. Invite small group reports.

key questions for us to ponder: Did Martha's confession mean she wholly accepted that death was unavoidable? Does her confession confirm her belief in life after death? Does her confession show that she has faith in the Life-Giver who sees people through the crisis of death? Was her confession of faith preparation for what Jesus said to her in verse 40? Based on verses 41-42, for whom was the sign intended?

What Else Would We Like to Know About Mary and Martha?

Adoring Jesus by Serving Him

The Gospel of John was written around the close of the first century. At that time, Christian service, called *diakonia* was an accepted form of ministry; and the servant, called *diakonos,* was recognized in some Christian communities as a ministerial office. Service included waiting on tables as a function of laying on hands. This is a helpful frame of reference for viewing one additional story about Mary and Martha appearing in the Gospel of John. It is a story about their serving Jesus. We find it in John 12:1-8.

The Scripture connects the timing of the sisters' service with the story in which their brother Lazarus was raised. We also see some characteristics of the sisters that remind us of those appearing in the pas-

Adoring Jesus
by Serving Him

Provide sheets of 8 ½" by 11" paper and have members divide their sheets in half, print "Diakonos" (servant) as the heading on the left side and "Diakonia" (service) as the heading on the right. Use dictionaries of New Testament words or other tools for further descriptions of the words. Have members write descriptions on their paper. Then tell them that there is a story of Mary and Martha in John 12:1-8 that demonstrates the meaning of the words.

Have the group read the story silently or divide the group in half with each half reading alternate verses.

On a piece of paper, have group members write Martha's name on the left side. On the right side write how she served. Repeat the same instructions for Mary.

 Look for similarities and differences between the roles of Mary and Martha in this story and their roles in Luke 10:38-42.

 Discuss why Mary and Martha should be referred to as *diakonos*.

 Using a commentary on the Gospel of John, explore reasons for Judas' objections.

 In the space provided, answer the question, What importance may we assign to Mary's actions in light of the emphasis in John's Gospel on mature faith?

Invite several group members to use creative movement or dance to show Mary's adoration. They may pattern their movements according to those needed to carry out her service as indicated in John 12:3. The group may accompany the move-ment by singing softly the song, "My Soul Gives You Glory, My Jesus."

sage from Luke we studied earlier. However, it contains some key differences.

Note that Judas the disciple did not object to Mary's adoration of Jesus through footwashing. In fact, it is possible that footwashing was part of the ritual of the early Christian community to which the Gospel writer belonged. So why was Judas objecting? Moreover, what importance may we assign to Mary's actions in light of Jesus' actions in John 13:14-17? What importance may we assign to Mary's actions in light of the emphasis in the Gospel of John on mature faith?

Mary and Martha As Discipleship Exemplars Today

Invite group members to identify present-day "Marys" and "Marthas" whose lives demonstrate attentive and devoted relationship with Jesus.

Ask group members to describe ways churches already help or could help people know Jesus Christ is with them in their struggles.

What Does it Mean For Me to Set Priorities to Welcome Jesus?

Invite the group into a time of open discussion, using the material found in the text.

Mary and Martha As Discipleship Exemplars Today

The stories of Mary and Martha provide a prism for viewing discipleship today. They invite us to consider who among us today takes time to intentionally listen to the Master Teacher. They invite us to consider how our faith communities make a space for people to struggle with their faith during times of crisis and to arrive at a deeply felt confession of faith. The examples of the footwashing Jesus commended to his disciples and Mary's footwashing invite us to consider the relationship between adoring Jesus, serving him, and serving one another. We are invited to consider those who are like Mary today and whose adoration of Jesus Christ leads them to mature discipleship even in ways appearing to be unpopular.

How Does What I Now Know About Mary and Martha Affect My Life and Faith?

What Does it Mean For Me to Set Priorities to Welcome Jesus?

As followers of Jesus, Mary and Martha set different priorities for how they welcomed Jesus into their home. Recall the way in which each one received him. Consider your own duties, chores, expectations, and responsibilities at home and elsewhere as well as what you consider distractions and why. Consider the extent to which you spend time in prayer and devotion with intentional focus on:

To close, have members select a partner and offer prayers for each other. To do this, invite the partners to share with each other requests for prayer. These request could be in the areas of setting priorities that would help them welcome Jesus into their everyday lives and maintaining and confessing their faith during hard times.

- getting in touch with God's concern for you;
- God's reaching out to you through Jesus Christ; and
- listening to God's direction for your life.

Consider ways in which you balance duties, chores, expectations, and responsibilities with time in prayer, in worship, and in Bible study.

What Does it Mean For Me to Examine My Faith?

We do not go through life without experiencing times of hardship or crisis. Consider the impact particular times of crisis had on your faith. Recall Martha's conversation with Jesus and her confession of faith during the death of Lazarus. Consider what her confession has to say to you.

What Does It Mean For Me To Adore and Serve Jesus?

We may find it easier to adore and serve Jesus in good times than in difficult times and circumstances. We may also find it easier to adore and serve Jesus in popular ways than in ways that others might consider too costly, too dirty, too demeaning, or even too ordinary. Mary and Martha's understanding of *diakonia* in John 12:1-7 invites us to consider:

● our personal understanding of *diakonia* (service) and how we engage in it now;

● what Mary and Martha as *diakonos* (servant) have to say to us personally about our future discipleship; and

● ways in which the song, "My Soul Gives You Glory, My Jesus," reflects Mary's, Martha's, and our own commitment to discipleship.

In Closing

What meanings did this lesson hold for you? What insights or learning did you gain? What surprised you? What assumptions or beliefs were challenged and/or reinforced? In what way(s) did you experience God as you moved through the lesson and learned about Mary and Martha?

Chapter Five

Nicodemus

CHOOSE FROM THE FOL-
LOWING ACTIVITIES TO
REFLECT ON NICODEMUS
AS JESUS' FOLLOWER.

Meet Nicodemus

● Introduce the biblical story
of Nicodemus using the
description found in the
text. The leader/teacher
may summarize this mater-
ial. Or group members
may read it aloud or
silently.

 Show the group
same-colored plac-
ards or 5" x 7"
pieces of paper with
descriptions of Nicodemus.
(Pharisee, Leader of the
Jews, Member of the San-
hedrin, and Teacher). The
signs will be used for a
later art activity.
Tell the group that the story
of Nicodemus appears only
in the Gospel of John. Also
mention that much of the
story appears in the second
section of John, often called
the "Book of Signs." Show
on placards or 5" x 7" signs:
"The Gospel of John," and
"The Book of Signs."
Choose a different color for
these signs than the one for
signs describing Nicodemus.
Keep the signs for a later art
activity.

What Does the Bible Say About Nicodemus?

Meet Nicodemus

Christians have retold the Bible story of
Nicodemus through singing.

The story of Nicodemus is found in the
Gospel of John. The Gospel characterizes him as a Pharisee and a leader of the
Jews (John 3:1). John 7:45-50 suggests
that he most likely was a member of the
Sanhedrin in Jerusalem. The Sanhedrin
was the Jewish governing body com-
prised of chief priests and Pharisees. The
Scripture draws further attention to
Nicodemus's elite status by identifying
him as a teacher of Israel. He was a
learned man and knew the story of God
and the historical sojourn of God's people in the Scripture we know as the Old
Testament. He was also an older man
(John 3:4).

Primary parts of Nicodemus's story
appear in the second section of John's
Gospel. We discovered in the previous
chapter on Mary and Martha that the second section of the Gospel is often called
the "Book of Signs." We will recall that
this section focuses on what Jesus

Invite group members into a process of exploring what there is to know about Nicodemus that would cause someone to remember him? Also invite them to explore Nicodemus as a seeker, a defender, and as the attendant. Show each of these descriptions on circular cards using a different color from the signs used earlier. These cards will be used for a later activity.

Nicodemus The Seeker

 Have the group read silently John 2:1-25.

 Discuss the impact of Jesus' signs on the people as told in John 2:11 and the impact of Jesus' signs on the people as told in John 2:23. Invite the group to enter Nicodemus's story by reading aloud John 3:2. Have them recall the time of Nicodemus's meeting with Jesus and Nicodemus's opening words. Also have them recount evidence in the verse showing that Nicodemus came on behalf of others.

● Invite the group to read aloud John 3:3.

Write the answer in the spaces provided as means of remembering this key information.

revealed to the world through his public ministry. Nicodemus's story does not contain any of the signs Jesus performed. Nonetheless, the signs are important to the account.

Nicodemus The Seeker

The story of Nicodemus begins in John 3:1-21. The foundation for the story is laid and the impact of the signs is discussed in John 2:1-25. Before the story of Nicodemus begins, John writes about the first of Jesus' signs in Cana of Galilee (John 2:1-12). Note the impact of Jesus' signs on his followers in John 2:11.

We discover in John 2:23 how the signs Jesus did in Jerusalem during the Passover festival affected people. As the story of Nicodemus begins, John gives the impression that Nicodemus was aware of the signs Jesus did. He had most likely been among the observers of these signs. On this basis, Nicodemus sought Jesus to interview him; he apparently came to Jesus on behalf of others. In John 3:2, we discover when Nicodemus came to see Jesus and how he began the conversation. Note what Nicodemus says that lets us know that he

Divide the group in half. Have half read aloud John 3:4. Have the other half read aloud John 3:5-8. Then invite the group to write the questions found in John 3:4 and summarize Jesus' response in the spaces provided.

 Ask: What was there about Nicodemus's acknowledgment of Jesus as a teacher that prompted Jesus' response? Why were Jesus' words so difficult for Nicodemus to understand?

Have the group read aloud John 2:24-25. Then have group members propose additional answers to the questions.
Ask: What does being born from above by water and the Spirit mean?

 Invite the group to read silently John 1:19-34. Then ask a group member to read aloud verse 31. Have another to read verses 32-33.

 Have small groups use a Bible dictionary, commentary on the Gospel of John, or other interpretation tools to gain further insights into the meaning of being born from above by water and the Spirit (John 3:5-8).

came on behalf of others.

Time of his visit:

His opening words:

Evidence he came on behalf of others:

Jesus' actual words:

The actual words of Jesus appear to be puzzling to Nicodemus. Out of his quandary, Nicodemus raises two specific questions in John 3:4 and receives a fur-

Discuss findings with the whole group. Ask the group to summarize the significance of water and the Spirit in the spaces provided.

 Invite the group to read aloud John 3:9 and then read silently the verses 11-16.
Ask group members to identify a key word that is repeated several times in the verses.

Discuss the importance of the word *believe*.

Have the group recall previous times and circumstances of hearing, reading, or reciting John 3:16. Then review the verse silently and recite it aloud.

Invite the group to read silently John 3:17-21 and John 3:2.

 Discuss the meaning of light and darkness as it relates to Nicodemus and the life of believers.

ther response from Jesus in verses 5-8 that proves equally as puzzling.

We might ask: What was there about Nicodemus's acknowledgment of Jesus as a teacher come from God that prompted Jesus' response? Why were Jesus' words so difficult for Nicodemus to understand? We discover one clue in John 2:24-25 about what Jesus already knew.
We discover the second clue by looking again at the central message in Jesus' response. Note the emphasis on more than intellectual and earthly knowledge about the kingdom of God. Jesus' answer is that Nicodemus and those he represents must be born from above by water and the Spirit. Why? The answer is linked with John's earlier story of John the Baptist, (John 1:19-34). Note in verse 31 the significance of water. Note in verses 32-33 the significance of the Spirit.

The significance of water:

The significance of the Spirit:

Nicodemus did not grasp the central message, because he and others were expecting another kind of Messiah. They were expecting an earthly Messiah who would save them from earthly captivity created by earthly powers. Consequently, Nicodemus raised the question: "How can these things be?" (John 3:9). In verses 11-15, he receives further clarification. One key word is repeated over and over in these verses. This key word is also central to the meaning of John 3:16, a Scripture that is familiar to, and even memorized by, many Christians today.

The Key Word
John 3:17-21 closes the account of Nicodemus' visit with Jesus. These verses draw our attention back to verse 2. They help us see John's contrast between darkness and light as descriptions of Nicodemus's visit and the life of believers.

What Else Would We Like to Know About Nicodemus?

From what we have already discovered about Nicodemus, we may say that he was a seeker after Jesus; but he was pretty cautious in going about it. This is not the end of the story, however. We find the rest of the story later in the Gospel of John.

Nicodemus the Defender

 Summarize happenings that led to Nicodemus becoming Jesus' defender.

Organize a mock meeting of the Sanhedrin.

Choose members to be chief priests and Pharisees, police, and Nicodemus.

Have the players huddle to read John 7:45-52 and to talk briefly through how they will act it out. Have remaining members read John 7: 40-44 and prepare to act this passage out prior to the Sanhedrin meeting.

Enact the people's scene followed by the Sanhedrin meeting.

Discuss what might have motivated Nicodemus to speak out. Also, discuss how the response of other chief priests and Pharisees might have affected him.

Nicodemus the Defender

On one occasion, Nicodemus became a defender of Jesus. Some important happenings led up to this action. The signs that Jesus did and the message of truth Jesus continued to proclaim in his public ministry led to ongoing animosity against him by the public. Jesus was persecuted (John 5:16). His life was in danger (John 5:18; 7:1). He was subject to arrest (John 7:30, 32, 44). At one point, the Temple police were actually sent by the high priests and Pharisees to arrest Jesus (John 7:32). However, the officers returned without him (John 7:45). We discover why in John 7:46.

According to the Gospel, the Pharisees attacked the reasoning of the Temple police and the credibility of Jesus (John 7:47-49). Nicodemus then spoke out. We discover what he said in John 7:50-51 and the response he received from fellow authorities in John 7:52.

Nicodemus the Attendant

 Have the group read silently John 19:38-42, and write in the space provided the name of the man whom Nicodemus helped to bury Jesus.

Discuss possible reasons for Nicodemus' role in Jesus' burial. Consider his visit with Jesus in John 3:1-21, his role as Jesus' defender in John 7:45-52, and the reason given for the secret burial noted in John 19:38.

 Seek further insights from Bible commentaries focused on John 19:38-42.

Nicodemus the Disciple

 Ask: Was Nicodemus really a disciple of Jesus?

 Use the text to contrast the findings in historical writings with the portrayal of Nicodemus in the Gospel of John.

Ask the group to draw conclusions on the importance of Nicodemus's story to their understanding of Christian discipleship.

Nicodemus the Attendant

The Gospel of John relates the unfolding events that resulted in Jesus' crucifixion in Chapters 18 and 19. The Gospel then tells about the circumstances of Jesus' burial. Two men attended to the body of Jesus. One of them was Nicodemus. We discover the name of the other attendant and an act of devotion Nicodemus carried out in John 19:38-42. Who did Nicodemus help to bury Jesus?

The two men held a common status in their society. Both were high-ranking, wealthy, and honorable Jewish leaders. John 19:38-39 suggests that they also held in common a particular kind of relationship with Jesus. Moreover, verse 38 gives us a reason for that kind of relationship.

Nicodemus the Disciple

In telling the story of Nicodemus, John never refers to him as a disciple. Even in the Scripture depicting his role in the burial of Jesus, Joseph of Arimathea is identified as a disciple; but Nicodemus is not so identified. Was Nicodemus in fact a disciple of Jesus?

Historical writings outside of the New Testament, called the Acts of Pilate, date back to the fourth century. These writings include stories of Nicodemus's baptism into the Christian faith, experiences of persecution and eventual banishment from Jerusalem. However, the story of Nicodemus in the Gospel of John is the one that stands today as a message to the world about the nature and hazards of caution taken in Christian discipleship.

What Nicodemus's Story Says About Discipleship Today

 Form small groups to discuss and write responses to each of the challenges appearing in the text.

Invite each small group to share their responses with the whole group.

What Nicodemus' Story Says About Discipleship Today

The story of Nicodemus offers a challenge to people today in every age or stage, including the older adult years. The story challenges us in at least five ways: (1) what it is about the Christian faith and the person of Jesus that attracts people; (2) what being "born from above" means and how believing in the Son of God relates to it; (3) what causes people to be "closet Christians" or to live cautiously the Christian faith; (4) when it is necessary for people to speak out on behalf of justice even at the risk of reprimand or reprisal; and (5) the acts of devotion to God through Jesus Christ that people carry out. Associated with this fifth challenge is the question: Is it ever too late to engage in an act of devotion?

How Does What I Now Know About Nicodemus Affect My Life and Faith?

Reflections on Faith and Discipleship

 Invite group members to cut out a variety of shapes from different colors of construction paper. Have them write on the shapes words or phrases telling what they learned about faith and discipleship from Nicodemus's story. Then create a mobile art object or "Informaton Tree."

Have ready a large bare tree branch anchored in a pot or a large potted plant.

Ask members to punch a hole in the shapes they cut out, then thread ribbon or string through the holes. Have them discuss the words or phrases on the shapes and hang the shapes on the branch or plant.

Add to the branch or plant the colored signs or placards shown earlier that describe Nicodemus.

Invite members to write in their journal about or discuss the five reflections on faith and discipleship appearing in the text.

Reflections on Faith and Discipleship

Recall that Nicodemus was attracted to Jesus because of the signs Jesus did. He also spoke with Jesus because he had some curiosity of his own that had been heightened by the curiosity of others. Recall now what attracted you to the Christian faith.

Recall that Nicodemus had difficulty comprehending what Jesus meant by being "born from above." Consider your own understanding and feelings about being "born from above." Consider also what you believe about the Son of God.

Recall that Nicodemus spoke with Jesus under secrecy of night and was an attendant at Jesus' burial in secrecy. Consider now any occasions in your life when your position, status, or esteem in another's eyes was or could have been jeopardized by your open stance as a Christian. Consider any jeopardy you currently face should you openly declare your Christian faith.

Recall that Nicodemus spoke out on Jesus' behalf in front of his fellow authorities in the Sanhedrin. He spoke out by raising a question about just treatment under the law. Recall now any occasion when you felt compelled to speak out about fairness on behalf of another person. Consider, as well, current instances of injustice where your voice is needed.

Recall that Nicodemus went with Joseph of Arimathea to bury Jesus. As part of the burial, Nicodemus displayed an act of devotion to Jesus. Explore now your own acts of devotion as well as where, when and why you do them. Answer the questions: What makes them acts of devotion? With whom may you enter into new forms of devotion now and as you grow older?

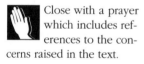 Close with a prayer which includes references to the concerns raised in the text.

In Closing

What meanings did this lesson hold for you? What insights or learning did you gain? What surprised you? What assumptions or beliefs were challenged and/or reinforced? In what way(s) did you experience God as you moved through the lesson and learned about Nicodemus?

Chapter Six

The Samaritan Woman

CHOOSE FROM THE FOLLOWING ACTIVITIES TO REFLECT ON THE SAMARITAN WOMAN AS JESUS' FOLLOWER.

Meet the Samaritan Woman

 Read in the Bible or from a Bible commentary about the events of conflict between the Samaritans and Jews described in Deuteronomy 26:1-26; 1 Kings 5-7; 2 Kings 17; Ezra 4; Nehemiah 4.

 To introduce the story of the Samaritan woman, divide chairs into three adjacent semicircles according to the regions of Judea in the south, Galilee in the north, and Samaria in between. Designate each section with a sign. Have group members sit in the sections for Judea and Samaria. In front of the semicircle representing Judea, place a sign on an empty chair that reads "The Temple of Jerusalem." In front of the semicircle representing Samaria, place a large barrel or container to represent Jacob's well and a bench beside it. Also place a sign on an empty chair that reads "Mount Gerizem."

What Does the Bible Say About the Samaritan Woman?

Meet the Samaritan Woman

The Samaritan woman was so named because of her ethnic origin. She was from the region of Samaria, the location of the Samaritan community. The region lies between Judea in the south and Galilee in the north. The Samaritan woman apparently lived in or near Sychar, a village near Shechem and close to a field Jacob gave to Joseph (Genesis 33:18-20; John 4:5). For this reason, she is sometimes called "the woman of Sychar."

Opinion differs on the actual name and location of the village. However, no dispute exists about the location of Jacob's well on which the people in the Shechem vicinity relied for their water supply. The well was located near the foot of Mount Gerizem. Mount Gerizem was the center of Samaritan worship. However, both the well and Mount Gerizem are important to the story of the Samaritan woman. Jesus met the Samaritan woman at this well. For this reason she is often called "the woman at the well."

Select a narrator for each of
the paragraphs in the text.
Then invite them to read the
paragraphs aloud.

A Matter of Ancestry

 Invite the first narra-
tor to read the first
paragraph aloud.

 Ask a group mem-
ber to use a Bible
dictionary to discov-
er the meaning of the Pentateuch.

 Invite the second
narrator to read the
second paragraph
aloud.

A Matter of Ancestry

The woman belonged to a people of
mixed marriages between the Jews and
the Babylonians. This situation came
about after the fall of the Northern Kingdom when thousands of Israelites were
departed into exile and the Babylonian
colonists came into central Palestine
around 721 B.C.E. Although both the Jews
and the Samaritans held to the Pentateuch, the Samaritans recognized only the
Pentateuch.

The Samaritans and the Jews built sepa-
rate places for the worship of God. Rely-
ing on their reading of the Pentateuch,
the Samaritans believed themselves to be
descendants of those whom Moses had
instructed to pronounce the blessings of
God on that mountain (Deuteronomy
26:1-26). The Jews believed Solomon had
been commissioned to build the true
place of worship in Jerusalem (1 Kings
5-7). Continuing differences in beliefs
about worship and political discord led
to ongoing enmity between the Jews and
the Samaritans (2 Kings 17; Ezra 4;
Nehemiah 4).

Invite reports from the volunteers who did advance preparation on conflict between the Samaritans and the Jews contained in 2 Kings 17; Ezra 4; Nehemiah 4).

 Invite the third narrator to read the third paragraph aloud.

The Jews considered the Samaritans foreigners and enemies. They typically avoided traveling through Samaria. No Jewish man would speak to a Samaritan woman, nor would he drink from a Samaritan's cup. The ancestry of the Samaritan woman and the strife between her people and the Jews set the stage for Jesus' conversation with her at Jacob's well.

A Scandalous Request

 Invite group members to read silently the beginning of the story of the Samaritan woman in John 4:1-7. Also, have them read silently the first paragraph in the text

 Ask group members in the Judean and Samaritan semi-circles to form pairs and dis-

A Scandalous Request

In Chapter 3 of John, we learned of Jesus' dialogue with Nicodemus, a respected elite Jewish male, residing in the territory of Judea. In John 4:1-42, Jesus speaks with the Samaritan woman whose ethnic cultural group was regarded by the Jews as a foreign enemy and whose name is never disclosed. Jesus' opening request and subsequent conver-

cuss from their perspectives as Jews or Samaritans the following:

What is the most appropriate route Jesus should take from Judea to Galilee? Why should Jesus travel through Samaria enroute to Galilee? What feelings or concerns do you have about Jesus' travel through Samaria enroute to Galilee in light of the historical relations between Jews and Samaritans? Why would Jesus want to go through Samaria, especially since it would be politically feasible for him to avoid it?

Invite the group to read silently the entire story of the Samaritan woman found in John 4:1-42.

Have a volunteer take the role of Jesus and another to take the role of the Samaritan woman. Ask them to enter the earlier prepared Jacob's well scene. Have them read aloud only the actual words of Jesus and the Samaritan woman found in verses 7-26.

 First, invite members to consider the passage silently. Then form small groups of three to four people to discuss the following questions:

sation with her were not indicative of acceptable behavior. By the standards of the day, his behavior was scandalous.

So why was Jesus in Samaria, especially since it would have been politically feasible for him to avoid it? What was he doing at Jacob's well? How did he happen to enter into conversation with the Samaritan woman? Our discovery of answers to the questions begins in John 4:1-7.

The conversation was perhaps as significant as it was scandalous because the Samaritan woman's trek to the well was during the hottest time of the day. We may ask: Why is it significant that she came there in the heat of the day? We may consider some obvious practical reasons. But we may also get some clues by looking again at the writer's intent in the second section of the Gospel of John in which the Samaritan woman's story appears. We have already explored this intent in the two previous chapters.

The Samaritan Woman As Jesus' Partner in Dialogue

After Jesus asked for the Samaritan woman's response to his request, the woman spoke with Jesus by asking him a series of questions (John 4:8-14). Some might consider the dialogue in these verses more along the lines of an argument than a harmonious discussion. But was this really the case? Was she being

Was the discussion between Jesus and the Samaritan woman an argument or a harmonious discussion? Was the Samaritan woman being sarcastic in verse 9? Was she really searching for some heartfelt answers to Jesus' presence?

Select group members to look in a Bible commentary on the Gospel of John for information on the meaning of "living water" in John 4:10, 13-14.

Have members consider silently, and then return to small groups of three or four to discuss the following: Was Jesus' message about "living water" puzzling to the Samaritan woman or was it an affront to her? Compare her responses in verses 11-12 and 13-14. What accounts for the change in her responses from one to the other?

Have the group re-read verses 16-18 aloud. Consult Bible commentaries or other interpretation materials for information about the appropriate etiquette to be shown in conversations between males and females of that day.

In the small groups, discuss the importance of the dialogue about the Samaritan

sarcastic in verse 9? Was she really searching for some heartfelt answers to Jesus' presence, his unusual request, and to his puzzling responses to her questions?

Her probing resulted in Jesus' references to "living water" which will cause those who receive it from him to "never be thirsty" (John 4:10, 13-14). Jesus also calls attention to the quality of this living water as the kind that "will become in them a spring of water gushing up to eternal life" (John 4:14b).

On the basis of her response in verses 11-12, we might assume that the depth of the message about living water in verse 10 was either puzzling or an affront to the Samaritan woman. However, the continuation of the dialogue results in a different response in verse 15 to Jesus' statement in verses 13-14 about "a spring of water gushing up to eternal life." This change of response raises the question: Why is it different?

Verse 16 brings a new dimension to the dialogue because it refers to the potential of someone other than the woman—her husband—as needing to be in the discussion. Although she answers in the negative (John 4:17a), Jesus' request to the woman to call her husband was an appropriate one according to the etiquette of the day.

We might also consider the request to be

woman's husband by answering the questions: Was Jesus calling attention to her sin? Was he giving her an opportunity to leave and not return? Was he attempting to let her know who he was? Or were there other reasons? Would Jesus' identity have been revealed without this part of the conversation? Was the Samaritan woman able to see who he was as a result of this part of the conversation?

 Have half the group read aloud verses 19-20. Have the other half read aloud verses 21-25. Then invite the small groups to answer the questions: What was the Samaritan woman's intent in verses 19-20? Why was it important for Jesus to respond as he did in verses 21-24?

 Read Deuteronomy 18:15. Consider the Samaritan woman's response in verses 21-24 in light of this verse as well as other reasons for her response.

 Have selected members consult Bible commentaries on the Gospel of John for further interpretations of Jesus' response in verses 21-24.

a strategic one. It is strategic because of the purpose Jesus had in mind for making the request in verse 16 and his later response in verse 17b. We might wonder if Jesus was attempting to call the Samaritan woman's attention to her sin. Or perhaps Jesus' focus really was not on moral laxity but, rather, on giving her opportunity to leave and not return. Perhaps Jesus' intent was part of his self-revelation as the One who has knowledge of all things as indicated in John 2:25.

Nonetheless, the discussion became intensely personal. On this basis, we might raise the question: Without this personal quality, would Jesus' identity have been revealed?

We might also ask: Did Jesus' emphasis on the woman's personal life function as a catalyst for her to see Jesus with new eyes?

The Samaritan woman's response to Jesus in verses 19-20 moves the dialogue to another level. It centers on the conflict between the Jews and the Samaritans about the proper place to worship God. She may have intended to divert discussion away from her personal life. Or she may have sought Jesus' perspectives on the place of worship that caused Jews to regard her and her people as foreigners and enemies.

Jesus' response in verses 21-24 places worship in a frame of reference larger than simply a place of worship. Her reply in verse 25 points to her longing for more clarity from the Messiah who "is coming." This reply may have had its origin in her own knowledge of Moses' prediction of an all-knowing prophet found in the Pentateuch (Deuteronomy 18:15). But she also may have considered the possibility that Jesus was this prophet. In this case, her response was designed to elicit further response from him. The discussion closes with Jesus' declaration of his messiahship (John 4:26).

What Else Would We Like to Know About the Samaritan woman?

Have selected group members read silently the opening two paragraphs in the text. Then have them read aloud John 4:40-42. Invite group discussion on the following and record responses on a large piece of paper: Why did the Samaritan woman tell others about her experience with Jesus? What is a disciple? What are key meanings of the story of the Samaritan woman for today? Assist the discussion of responses by using the questions appearing at the section end of the text.

The Samaritan woman proved to be unafraid to talk with Jesus. Moreover, the experience she had with Jesus at Jacob's well made her unafraid to testify about it to people in the city (John 4:39). Her testimony resulted from what Jesus told her during their time together as partners in dialogue.

But it also meant that during the dialogue, she had to hear what Jesus told her in order to be able to tell others about it. Her witness had a profound effect on others as noted in John 4:40:

Her name as a witness for Jesus was never revealed. She was never identified as a disciple of Jesus. Yet she became a catalyst for other Samaritans seeking

Jesus, hearing what he had to say, and from his message, coming to know him as "the Savior of the world" (John 4:40-42).

Jesus' Outreach and Desire for Response Today

The Gospel storyteller provides a message today of Jesus' intent to minister beyond the boundaries of acceptable social convention. His outreach extended beyond geographical, cultural, and gender barriers. It extended from "chosen people" to "rejected people," from likely people to unlikely people, from men to women. His ministry was to all. Consequently, his journey through rather than around "enemy" territory was what he had to do (John 4:4).

The Gospel storyteller also provides a message today of the power of Jesus to change the lives of people when they heed his request to respond to his presence, talk with him, and come to know and believe who he is. Moreover, the Gospel storyteller provides a message today of the self-propelling need of people who know and believe Jesus to tell somebody else, "I want you to know what happened to me!" In this way, they become witnesses for Jesus.

But the storyteller leaves us today to struggle with the questions: From whom is Jesus seeking a response to his presence today? What are the geographical, cultural, and gender barriers today that

Jesus wants torn down? How does Jesus' invitation get extended across geographical, cultural, and gender barriers today? How do people move toward and arrive at belief in Jesus Christ? Who are the unnamed witnesses today? Who are the women witnesses? Who may the unnamed witnesses yet be?

How Does What I Now Know About the Samaritan Woman Affect My Life and Faith?

Consider your first experience of Jesus' presence in your life or of your becoming aware of who he is. Describe ways in which the Samaritan woman's experience of Jesus was similar to or different from your own. Recall in detail what your experience was like:

- describe when and where it happened
- recall your thoughts and anything you said aloud
- recall your feelings

Consider any questions you have raised in the past about who Jesus is. Recall any answers you received to the questions as well as how you received the answers. Call to mind, as well, any unanswered past questions and new questions. Consider how you may receive answers to these questions.

Consider where and to whom you have already witnessed or yet may witness

• Invite group members into a journal writing process or open discussion of the following:

 Identify with the Samaritan woman by taking her role. On this basis, review what it was like moving through the experience with Jesus.

 Now from your own perspective, summarize the meaning of the story of the Samaritan woman for you today.

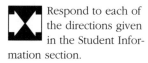 Respond to each of the directions given in the Student Information section.

about who you know Jesus to be:

- in your family
- in your church
- in your community
- in places across geographical, cultural, and gender boundaries

In Closing

 Invite the group to use the questions found in the text to reflect on the group's experience of the lesson.

Observe a moment of silence and close the session with a benediction.

In Closing

What meanings did this lesson hold for you? What insights or learning did you gain? What surprised you? What assumptions or beliefs were challenged and/or reinforced? In what way(s) did you experience God as you moved through the lesson and learned about the Samaritan woman?

Chapter Seven

Thomas

CHOOSE FROM THE FOL-
LOWING ACTIVITIES TO
REFLECT ON THOMAS AS
JESUS' DISCIPLE.

Meet Thomas

Begin by asking the group to comment on what they already know about Thomas. Some leading questions may be: What do you already know about who he was and what he was like? From where did you get your impressions about Thomas? When?

Organize a panel of four persons to present a preliminary depiction of Thomas. To prepare for the panel assign each panel member as facilitator of a small group. Tell them that the job of the small group is to discover specific information about Thomas as indicated below. They are also to collaborate together on how to present the information they have discovered. They may also decide to join the panelist in presenting their information. Some ideas of presentation might include simply telling the information, commenting on it, dramatizing it, or presenting pictures of it.

What Does The Bible Say About Thomas?

Meet Thomas

Thomas was the seventh of the twelve disciples whom Jesus appointed and named apostle (Matthew 10:3; Mark 3:18; Luke 6:15; John 11:16). The fourth Gospel not only identifies him by the name *Thomas* but also as "the twin" (John 11:16; 20:24; 21:2). The Greek word for *twin* is *didymos*. The Greek word is used in the King James Version of the Bible, and is perhaps the name by which Thomas was called by Greek-speaking Christians.

No information appears in the Gospel of John or in the other Gospels about Thomas' twin, or why he is so named. Likewise, we do not find in John's Gospel or the other Gospels any mention of his family or the town or region from which he came.

An apocryphal writing called The Acts of Thomas, dating back to the third century A.D., suggests that Thomas was Hebrew and a carpenter. This writing also contains material about Thomas's missionary journey to India. Although this informa-

Ask one panel member and her or his small group to read about Jesus' appointment of Thomas as a disciple and naming him as apostle in Matthew 10:3; Mark 3:18; Luke 6:15; John 11:16.

Ask one panel member and her or his small group to read Bible verses, including John 11:16; 20:24; and 21:2, in which Thomas is referred to a "the twin." Then, discover from a Bible dictionary or commentary additional information about Thomas's identification as "The Twin beyond what appears in the text.

 Have one panel member and his or her small group discover from a Bible dictionary, commentary or other interpretation tools what apocryphal writings are, what the Acts of Thomas says about Thomas, and what impressed you about what was revealed.

Have one panel member and his or her small group discover from a Bible dictionary, commentary or other interpretation tools the difference between a disciple and an apostle and compare them with understandings group members have held about each. At the conclusion of the panel planning time, invite the panel members to share their information.

tion is largely regarded as legend, there exists a Christian denomination named after Thomas (Mar Thoma Church) in south India from the very early stage of the Christian era. We rely on information about Thomas and his journey as a disciple of Jesus appearing in the Gospel of John. In fact, this information is unique to this Gospel.

A Time to Speak Out

Ask the group to read silently John 11:1-16, or divide into two groups with each group reading alternate verses.

Invite volunteers to role-play the scene depicted in the Scripture. Then guide the group in discussing: If you were one of the disciples, what would you have done in that situation?

Have the entire group read aloud verses 16-17. Ask the group members to read silently the text and write responses called for in the spaces provided.

Guide the group in discussing: What did you discover about Thomas in the passage? What does the passage tell us about discipleship and apostleship? What does Thomas's specific role tell us about discipleship and apostleship? What does the passage tell us about who Jesus is? What did it mean for Thomas to speak out? What were the consequences of his speaking out? What other questions or comments would you offer on this part of Thomas's story?

A Time to Speak Out

One part of Thomas's story appears in John 11:1-16. The Gospel writer refers to Thomas for the first time in this passage. The passage reveals Thomas's identity as a disciple and highlights what Thomas did that distinguished him from the other disciples. What did he do?

We will recall from the earlier session on Mary and Martha that the two sisters had sent a message to Jesus from their home in Bethany, a village in Judea. The message told Jesus that their brother Lazarus was ill. At the time Jesus received the message, he had left a difficult situation that involved him in Jerusalem. Jesus crossed the Jordan River to the place where John had been baptizing (John 10:22-42). The Jordan River was also the place where Jesus himself had been baptized by John (Mark 1:9-11).

Two days after receiving the message, Jesus announced to his disciples that, together, they would go to Judea (John 11:7). It was winter (John 10:22) and the journey promised to be a lengthy one on foot. But the real concern was the danger such a trip posed for Jesus. The disciples expressed concern for Jesus' safety (John 11:8). John 11:12 tells us that in the conversation about the trip, the disciples gave Jesus a plausible excuse for not going to Judea. But as stated in John 11:14-15, Jesus made plain his decision.

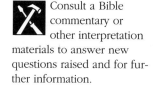 Consult a Bible commentary or other interpretation materials to answer new questions raised and for further information.

The excuse provided by the disciples:

Jesus' Decision:

In verse 16, we discover that Thomas responded to Jesus' decision with an appeal of his own. The appeal was not to Jesus. Some might consider what he proposed as courageous. Others may think that it reflects startling pessimism. After Thomas spoke, the story scene shifts, and we discover by the unfolding story in John 11:17 that Jesus and the disciples did not stay across the Jordan.

The intended audience for Thomas's appeal:

What Thomas said in his appeal:

A courageous or pessimistic appeal:

What happened after the appeal:

A Time for Questioning

 Ask the group to read silently John 14:1-7. Or divide into two groups with one group reading the words of Jesus and the other group reading Thomas's words.
● Guide the group in discussing: If you were one of the disciples, what would you have done in that situation?

Have the entire group read aloud verse 5. Invite the

A Time for Questioning
Another part of Thomas's story appears in John 14:1-7. The specifics of the story took place a short while before Jesus' arrest and crucifixion. In the company of his disciples, Jesus had already foretold Judas Iscariot's betrayal of him (John 13:21-26), and Peter's denial of him (John 13:36-38).

At the beginning of Chapter 14, the Gospel writer presents Jesus' opening words of farewell to his disciples. These

group to read silently the text and write responses called for in the spaces provided.

 Guide the group in discussing: What did you discover about Thomas in the passage? What does the passage tell us about discipleship and apostleship? What does Thomas's specific role tell us about discipleship and apostleship? What does the passage tell us about who Jesus is? What did it mean for Thomas to question Jesus? What were the consequences of his questioning? What other questions or comments would you offer on this part of Thomas's story?

words begin the section in the Gospel known as Jesus' first farewell discourse to the disciples (John 14:1-31). Through his words, Jesus declared to his disciples forthrightly, honestly, and with compassion that in the face of his impending death, they need not worry because he was going to prepare a place for them (John 14:1-3). In verse 4, Jesus adds an important reminder of what he assumed the disciples already knew.

The reminder:

Just as Thomas had been the earlier spokesperson for the disciples, he became so once again. He spoke in response to Jesus' reminder. His response was in the form of a question. We find his response in John 14:5:

What Else Would We Like to Know About Thomas?

A Time of Doubt

 Ask the group to read silently John 20:19-29. Or divide into two groups with each group reading alternate verses.

 Invite volunteers to role-play the scene depicted in verses 24-29.

A Time of Doubt
We have discovered that the Gospel of John presents Thomas as an important spokesperson for the disciples. But in the part of his story found in John 20:24-29, Thomas speaks for himself. We find in this passage the familiar incident that has resulted in references to him as "Doubting Thomas." Why is this so?

Ask group members to identify with Thomas and, on this basis, discuss: What was Thomas feeling and thinking that caused him to respond as he did?
Then have the entire group read aloud verses 28-29.

 Have group members read silently the text and write responses called for in the spaces provided.

 Guide the group in discussing: What did you discover about Thomas in the passage? What does the passage tell us about discipleship and apostleship? What does Thomas's specific role tell us about discipleship and apostleship? What does the passage tell us about who Jesus is? What did it mean for Thomas to express doubt? What were the consquences of his expression of doubt? What other questions or com-ments would you offer on this part of Thomas' story?

 Consult a Bible commentary or other interpretation materials to answer new questions raised and for further information.

We can guess that after the crucifixion of Jesus the world of the disciples had caved in. The One who had introduced them to a way of life they had not known before was gone. They were without their close companion, leader, teacher, and spiritual guide.

Because of the hostile environment surrounding the crucifixion and negative attitudes toward Jesus' followers, the disciples lived in fear for their lives. They withdrew behind locked doors (John 20:19). But Jesus appeared in the midst of them, assured them of his identity, greeted them, commissioned them to go forth in ministry, and entreated them to receive the Holy Spirit (John 14:26). For some unknown reason, Thomas was not with the other disciples when Jesus appeared to them. He learned about appearance from them. He was puzzled by what they said to the extent that he wanted proof in order to believe.

The proof Thomas wanted:

We discover in John 20:26-28 that Thomas received the proof he needed from Jesus, who responded precisely to Thomas's expressed doubts and invited him to put his doubts to the test. When Thomas did so, he was able to confess his faith (John 20:28). In fact, his confession is understood by Bible scholars as the earliest one of its kind.

Thomas's confession of faith:

But as told in verse 29, Jesus invited Thomas to reflect on the difference between seeing through everyday human eyesight and seeing through eyes of faith. Some may consider Thomas as the doubter who missed the mark as a disciple. Others may think of him as an honest follower who did not fear seeking answers to what he did not understand. Still others may call him a catalyst for disclosing who Jesus is.

Was Thomas a doubter who missed the mark or was Thomas a honest follower?

Was Thomas a catalyst for disclosing who Jesus is?

A Time of Obedience

 Ask the group to read silently John 21:1-14. Or divide into two groups with each group reading alternate verses.

 Ask volunteers to role-play the scene depicted in the Scripture. Or have group members draw a picture of the scene, put Thomas's name beside his figure in the picture, and write the verse(s) that highlight the disciple's obedience. Have members show their pictures and tell the verse(s) they chose.
Invite the entire group to read verses 5-6.

A Time of Obedience
In Chapter 21, known as the epilogue or appendix to the Gospel of John, Jesus appears once again to the disciples. Thomas is among the seven in the group who witness this appearance. We discover the account of this event in verses 1-14. In this account, Jesus appears to the seven by the Sea of Tiberias at sunrise after the seven had an unsuccessful time of night fishing. In reading the account, we discover that Jesus appeared on the beach, made a queried comment about their catch, and gave them some fishing instructions. In some respects, the story functions as a sequel to Jesus' call to the first disciples (Mark 1:16-20). But it also differs in significant respects. We also dis-

Ask group members to read silently the text and write responses called for in the spaces provided.

 Guide the group in discussing: What did you discover about Thomas in the passage? What does the passage tell us about discipleship and apostleship? What does Thomas's specific role tell us about discipleship and apos- tleship? What does the pas- sage tell us about who Jesus is? What did it mean for Thomas to be obedient to Jesus' invitation? What were the consequences of his obedience? What other questions or comments would you offer on this part of Thomas's story?

 Consult a Bible commentary or other interpretation materials to answer new questions and for further information.

Jesus Speaks Through Thomas to Us Today

 Guide the group in discussing: From our study of Thomas, how would you now describe Thomas? How does our understanding of Thomas connect with our understanding of being Christians today?

cover that Thomas has a part in this post Resurrection story that is quite different from his previous roles.

Some may consider Thomas as not really pivotal to the story. Others may think that the Gospel writer was showing Thomas's obedience to Jesus out of his full knowing, along with the others, of the message and the messenger.

Was Thomas unimportant to the story or was he an obedient follower?

Was Thomas and the others catalysts for disclosing who Jesus is?

Jesus Speaks Through Thomas to Us Today

The character of Thomas that prevails for many today is that of the doubter. Because of his doubt, people sometimes tend to be critical of him. Yet it may be that, in Thomas, we see a range of quali- ties that are found in Christians today, especially when we are confronted with experiences we do not understand and losses that bring us to the brink of despair.

What Does What I Now Know About Thomas Affect My Life and Faith?

When and How Do I Speak Out?

 Invite the group to write in their journals or discussion in small groups, using the material found in the text.

Have group members read and respond to the questions raised in each section.

Ask members to write down key insights resulting from their responses to the sections.

 If group members wrote in their journals, invite them to share with the group one key insight they gained in each of the sections. If the group engaged in small group discussion, ask a recorder for each group to summarize and report insights to the whole group.

When and How Do I Speak Out?

Recall that at one point in Thomas's sojourn as a disciple, he felt compelled to take on the role of leader and to speak out for right action, in spite of its potential risks. This part of his story raises several issues regarding the way in which we as Christians make decisions. The first of these issues regards our conscience. Our questions to ourselves are: When I become aware of the needs of others and difficult social and political situations requiring action by me and others around me, what helps me distinguish what is right to say or do? In what situation(s) am I now being called to speak out of my conscience?

The second issue has to do with compassion. Our questions to ourselves are: When I become aware of the needs of others and difficult social and political situations requiring action by me and others around me, am I able to put myself in the situation of the ones in need? In what situation(s) am I now being called to speak out of my compassion?

The third issue concerns commitment. Our questions to ourselves are: When I become aware of needs of others and difficult social and political situations requiring action by me and others around me, do I feel a sense of obligation to respond in helpful ways? In what situation(s) am I now being called to speak out of my commitment?

When Have I Been a Doubting Disciple?

Recall that Thomas had great difficulty believing in Jesus' real presence after the crucifixion until he had tangible proof of it. This part of his story invites us to consider: At what time(s) in my life have I doubted Jesus' presence with me? What caused my doubt?

Am I an Obedient Follower?

Recall that Thomas witnessed Jesus' appearance on the beach by the Sea of Tiberias. He also heard and followed Jesus' instructions in cooperation with the other disciples because they knew who he was. This part of Thomas's story invites us to consider: On which side is Jesus calling me to "cast my net"? How may I respond?

In Closing

What meanings did this lesson hold for you? In what way(s) did you experience God as you moved through the lesson and learned about Thomas?